Port of
SOUTHAMPTON
in the
60s & 70s

Port of
SOUTHAMPTON
in the
60s & 70s

CAMPBELL McCUTCHEON

AMBERLEY

Canberra, 19 August 1972.

First published 2009

Amberley Publishing
Cirencester Road, Chalford,
Stroud, Gloucestershire, GL6 8PE

www.amberleybooks.com

Copyright © Campbell McCutcheon 2009

The right of Campbell McCutcheon to be identified as the Author
of this work has been asserted in accordance with the
Copyrights, Designs and Patents Act 1988.

British Library Cataloguing in Publication Data.
A catalogue record for this book is available from the British Library.

ISBN 978 1 84868 286 3

Typeset in Sabon LT
Typesetting and Origination by Fonthill
Printed in Great Britain

Contents

Introduction 7

Chapter 1 The Age of the Liner 9

Chapter 2 The Changing Face of Cargo Ships 75

Chapter 3 Red Funnels & Other Ferries 95

Chapter 4 Cables, Tugs, Explorers & Small Ships 109

Chapter 5 The White Ensign 121

The brand-new, Liberian-registered *Brazilian Marina* (150,518grt) on 8 August 1976.

Introduction

This is my second book on the Port of Southampton. The first, *Port of Southampton* (ISBN 9781848680616), is more of a general history of the port from its earliest origins up to the present day. I used some of my collection of old photographs and postcards to illustrate *Port of Southampton* and I know from feedback received that many people took pleasure from the memories contained within the images. I was lucky enough last year to purchase a large collection of photographs all taken by one man on numerous trips to Southampton docks over the period from the late 1950s to the late 1970s. With over 1,000 images to choose from, the choice of what to put in and what to leave out has been difficult, but I hope I have shown a representative selection of ships that you could have seen any week of the year over the period from the 1960s through to the late 1970s. Despite having many superb images from this period of the docks and the ships that sailed from it, I have deliberately chosen to showcase the images of the one unknown photographer whose work you see in front of you. He had great foresight in taking these pictures, but also in writing on the reverse of each and every one the ship and date the photo was taken.

The port, like every port in the UK, saw great changes in the period covered in this book, from the great seamen's strike of 1966, which effectively shut the British shipping industry with many ships trapped in port for the duration, to the phenomenal growth of containerisation from the late 1960s onwards. In addition, the closing of Southampton's ship repair yards and the rebuilding of the inner docks, which, by the mid-1970s, were derelict again as the ferry services from Southampton were either moved to Portsmouth or were unsuccessful and stopped.

The intention of this book is not to be a history book but more to put into the public domain some of the images taken by an unknown photographer, who loved ships even more than I do.

As always, writing a book is never a solitary pursuit and some people need to be thanked for their help. First and foremost must be the man who took these images and collected them together – he remains unknown to me but he must be thanked for the great service he did in cataloguing the changing face of the port of Southampton; second is Rick Cox, who introduced me to the collection and who let me pick a few thousand images of not just Southampton but also the Port of London and the River Thames; third and fourth are my wife and daughter, who have lost me for a few weeks as I have written up the captions to the fantastic pictures you will see in the following pages. Thank you to you all!

Campbell McCutcheon
June 2009

The Israeli MV *Persimmoncore*, 27 October 1968.

CHAPTER I

The Age of the Liner

Since the mid-nineteenth century Southampton has been a liner port, and can claim to have a longer association with the true ocean liner, as opposed to the cruise ship, than any other port of the world. The first Royal Mail Steam Packet Company's sailings began in 1842, and the port has seen a constant stream of ships leaving for harbours around the world, including New York, Cape Town, Hong Kong, Rio de Janeiro, Buenos Aires, Sydney and Auckland. There was a time when liners left every day for every corner of the world, but since the loss of the Union Castle Line's mail service in 1977, the mantle of liner voyages has been left to Cunard, with the *Queen Elizabeth 2* on the transatlantic route. With the building of the new liner *Queen Mary 2*, it seems that Cunard will be operating a transatlantic passenger service well into the 2020s, continuing the trend for at least two more decades. Contained within the next few pages are just a selection of liners that sailed to and from Southampton in the 1960s and 1970s, including some of the most famous ships afloat, not just from Cunard, but from British India, P&O, Royal Mail Lines, the United States Lines, French Line and Aznar Line.

In May 1952 a new record-breaker entered Southampton for the first time. She was the glamorous SS *United States*, America's new flagship ocean liner. Heavily subsidized by the US Navy and capable of conversion to a troopship in a day, she is still the fastest liner afloat. She was withdrawn from service in 1969 but still remains in a Philadelphia dock. Up for sale at the time of writing, she may be scrapped soon.

14 September 1957 and the six-year-old *Arcadia* of P&O leaves Southampton. On the right is a Red Funnel steamer, while, on the left, the huge Stothert & Pitt cranes dominate the sky. *Arcadia* was launched on 14 May 1953 at John Brown's on the Clyde, with a maiden voyage from London to Sydney via Bombay, Colombo and Melbourne on 14 February 1954.

The British India Steam Navigation Co. was at one time the largest owner of ships in the UK. By the 1950s it was a part of P&O and until the 1960s many of the contracts for troop transport to India and the Far East went to BI.

Here, MV *Dilwara* (12,555grt, 1936) is in port on 14 September 1957.

Less than a year old, *Oriana*'s corn livery is already looking weather-worn after a season of voyages to the Antipodes. This view dates to 20 July 1961. *Oriana* was Orient Line's last liner and entered service in November 1960 for a short voyage to Lisbon with the Association of British Travel Agents' annual convention aboard.

Another ship barely a year old when this photo was taken on 20 July 1961, was the Union Castle Line's RMS *Windsor Castle*. At 37,640grt she was the largest ship on the South Africa mail run. Built on the Mersey at Cammell Laird's she was to have a long life, although post-1977 much of it was spent at anchor off Piraeus before she was sent to Alang, India, for breaking in 2005. The tender *Calshot*, now owned by Southampton City Council, is to the right.

Elders & Fyffe's banana boat *Sulaco* (1,602grt, 1931) was a frequent visitor to the port. Shown here on 20 July 1961.

The Bibby Line troopship SS *Oxfordshire* on 20 July 1961.

Cunard's RMS *Queen Elizabeth*, at the time the world's largest ship at 83,673 tons, berthed at Southampton's Ocean Terminal on 20 July 1961. She's about to set off for New York again, and one tug is at her bow to pull her out of her berth, while another, *Romsey*, is at her stern.

Above: A survivor of the Second World War, when she was used as a troopship, *Strathmore* is resplendent in her all-over white livery on 20 July 1961, while berthed at the Western Docks. In 1961 she was converted from a two-class ship, with 525 first-class and 500 tourist passengers, to a 1,250-passenger, one-class ship. In the summer of 1963 she was sold to John Latsis and renamed *Marianna Latsis* for use on the Karachi-Mecca pilgrimage run. Renamed again in 1966 as *Henrietta Latsis*, she was scrapped at Spezia, Italy, in 1969.

Left: Shown here in her green livery on 9 July 1964, Cunard's *Mauretania* of 1939 was built on the Mersey at Cammell Laird's yard and entered service just before the start of the Second World War. Spending her war years as a troopship, she was sent cruising in the 1960s but was sold for scrapping in November 1965 and left for Inverkeithing, Scotland, to be dismantled. It was in 1962 that *Mauretania* acquired this livery.

Pendennis Castle (28,582grt, built 1958) having just berthed on 9 July 1964. On 23 April 1976 she made her last sailing to South Africa. Sold to Hong Kong, after a period of idleness, she was scrapped in 1980.

The 1936 Harland & Wolff-built RMS *Stirling Castle*, with *Windsor Castle* ahead, on 2 August 1964. In 1966 *Stirling Castle* was sold for scrap, sailing from Southampton to Mihara, Japan, and arriving there on 3 March.

Left and below: On 2 August 1964, two Dutch liners were in port. Top is the *Willem Ruys*, which went on to become the ill-fated *Achille Lauro* of Lauro Lines, while below is the *Oranje*, of 1939. Both ships sailed the routes to Indonesia from Rotterdam via the Suez Canal.

Photographed from Mayflower Park on 9 July 1964 is the United States' nuclear-powered ship *Savannah*. Entering service in 1962, *Savannah* was not a commercial success and lasted a mere ten years before she made her final commercial voyage. Built at a cost of almost $47M, and one of only four nuclear-powered cargo ships, *Savannah* was destined to become a museum ship. She is currently laid up after much work to remove her radioactive material.

Built in 1940 as the freighter *Mormacmail* for Moore McCormack Line, the ship was taken over by the US Navy and renamed *Long Island*. After the war she was sold and converted to the passenger ship *Nelly*, then renamed *Seven Seas* in 1953. In 1955 she was chartered to the Europe-Canada Line. She sailed from Bremen via Southampton and Le Havre to Quebec and Montreal and is shown here on 2 August 1964. In June 1965, she caught fire and was towed to Newfoundland. Repaired, she made her last voyage in September 1966 and was sold to Rotterdam University to be used as a students' hostel.

The ex-Pacific Steam Navigation Co.'s *Reina del Mar* in her Union Castle livery, albeit badly needing a repaint, on 27 April 1966. Managed by Union Castle and used on cruises, she was eventually purchased by them in 1973. For many people she was the quintessential cruise ship and the first ship many sailed on. Scrapped in 1975, she was a great loss to the fledgling cruise industry in Britain.

A superb view of RMS *Windsor Castle* entering port on 27 April 1966. *Windsor Castle* was one of Cammell Laird's finest ships, after the 1939 *Mauretania*, and was launched on the Mersey on 23 June 1959, watched by a crowd of tens of thousands. After being sold when Union Castle disposed of their passenger fleet in 1977, she became a luxury accommodation ship in Jeddah.

The South African *SA Oranje* was constructed in 1948 as *Pretoria Castle*. Named by Mrs Issie Smutts, wife of the then South African president, she slipped down the ways at Harland & Wolff's, Belfast, on 19 August 1947. Shown here outward bound on 29 April 1966, she had been transferred to South African ownership on 1 January 1966. After 187 voyages, she arrived for scrapping at Kaohsuing on 2 November 1975.

SA Vaal was built in 1961 and is shown here on 21 May 1966. Launched as *Transvaal Castle* at Clydebank and entering service in 1961, she was transferred to Safmarine in 1966. She became the *Festivale* for Carnival Cruises, a company which has now expanded to include many famous lines including P&O, Cunard, Holland America and Princess Cruises.

Sitmar's *Fairstar* on 21 May 1966, with Royal Mail Lines' *Andes* behind her. Originally a trooper for Bibby Line and launched as SS *Oxfordshire*, she was initially chartered in 1963 by Sitmar for six years but purchased outright in 1964. In that year a dispute with the shipbuilder converting her saw her move to Harland & Wolff's in Southampton for completion. She sailed on her maiden voyage to Australia in May 1964. Ten years later she became the first dedicated Australian cruise ship and was sold with the rest of the Sitmar fleet to P&O who retained her name. In 1997 she left Australia for the last time on a journey to India for breaking.

Fyffe's *Golfito* was built on the Clyde by Alexander Stephens at Linthouse in 1949, and was one of a pair of ships that were designed for passenger service as well as for the banana trade. She is shown here on 21 May 1966.

Sightseers take a tour of the Western Docks on 21 May 1966. The Harland & Wolff-constructed *Canberra* is getting some attention as they sail past on the *Skylark*.

Launched on 14 December 1954 on the Clyde as *Ivernia*, the second of the *Sylvania* sisters was renamed as *Franconia* on 1 January 1963. She was the third Cunarder to have this name and is shown here on 21 May 1966.

Less than a month after the image on page 18, *Reina del Mar* looks resplendent on 21 May 1966, freshly painted, but she was soon to spend a long time laid up during the Seamens' Strike of 1966. Behind the *Reina del Mar* is RMS *Edinburgh Castle*.

Built in 1957, the Holland America Line's *Statendam* is shown here on 20 July 1966.

Inward bound, and with five tugs bringing her in on 20 July 1966, is the *United States*, America's Blue Riband winner and capable of over 40kt with all eight boilers functioning. Today she lies derelict and with her interiors sold off in the 1980s; she is but a shell of the liner shown here. The author has a cabin telephone from aboard the SS *United States* in his collection of ocean liner memorabilia.

The Seamen's Strike was to have a huge impact on British shipping. Southampton was absolutely full of ships, all destined to be laid up for months. It was the beginning of the end of the British merchant fleet. Laid up here on 20 July 1966 are, from left to right, the *Good Hope* and *Southampton Castles*, both only a year old, with the *SA Oranje* on this view taken from Mayflower Park.

It is 6 August 1967 and P&O's *Arcadia* is dressed in flags while the Chandris Line's *Australis* is in the process of being painted in this view of the Western Docks.

A close-up view of the Chandris Line's SS *Australis* being repainted, a lighter at her side.

The ten-year-old Dutch *Prins der Nederlanden* on 6 August 1967.

Built at Monfalcone for Cosulich, an Italian line, and originally named *Vulcania*, she was transferred to Italia in 1937. Purchased by the Siosa Line, part of the Grimaldi group, in 1965, *Vulcania* was renamed as *Caribia*. On 23 September 1972 *Caribia* hit a rock and was laid up. In 1974 she was scrapped in Taiwan. Because of soot on her aft decks, a funnel extension (shown here) was added to the ship while in Siosa ownership.

Above and left: The date is 16 August 1967, and *Queen Mary* is berthed at the Ocean Terminal, just a month before she set sail on her 1,000th voyage and her last-ever transatlantic trip from New York to Southampton.

Photographed on the same day is the Spanish steamer *Montserrat*. Built in 1945 as *Wooster Victory* in California, she became a Sitmar ship in 1950 and was sold to the Cia Transatlantica Espanola in 1957 and renamed *Montserrat*. She had six more years of service ahead of her before being broken at Castellon in 1973.

The Union Castle liner RMS *Pendennis Castle* berthed in the Western Docks on 16 August 1967.

Making her maiden voyage in wartime, *Andes* is shown here on a rainy 3 September 1967. She became one of Royal Mail Lines' best-known cruise ships and was sold for scrap to Belgian shipbreakers at Ghent in 1971 at a price of £300,000. *Andes* had steamed 2,750,000 miles in her 31 years of service.

Originally built as a freighter in San Francisco, but converted while building into an escort aircraft carrier, loaned to Britain and named HMS *Attacker*, *Fairsky* was capable of carrying eighteen aircraft and saw escort duties in the North Atlantic, Mediterranean and Pacific. Retired in 1946 and laid up, she was sold in 1947 and her armament and flight deck removed. Part way through this work, she was sold again to Sitmar and converted into *Fairsky*. Work was not completed until December 1957 when she sailed for Genoa. As a Sydney-based cruise ship she hit a wreck in 1977 and was sold for scrap in 1978 after burning out while a floating hotel in the Phillipines.

Built for the Orient Line in 1950, *Oronsay* is being painted on 3 September 1967, two small barges close to her containing the scaffolding, the front one with three painters. She is being loaded with cargo for her next voyage.

Leaving on her last transatlantic to New York on 16 September 1967, *Queen Mary* would return on the 27th and would remain in Southampton until she was sold to the city of Long Beach for $3,350,000 in November that year.

Another ship that would leave Southampton for the last time in September 1967 was Union Castle's *Capetown Castle*. Built in 1938 in Belfast, she survived the war to sail to Italy for scrapping a few days after this view was taken on 16 September 1967.

Barrow-built at Vickers Armstrong's yard for P&O, *Himalaya* prepares to sail on 20 September 1967.

Edinburgh Castle in the Western Docks, viewed from Mayflower Park on 20 September 1967.

Elders & Fyffe's *Camito* is berthed in the Western Docks on 20 September 1967 after a voyage from the West Indies.

A stern view of *Himalaya* taken on the same day in Southampton's Western Docks.

Queen Elizabeth arrived in on 20 September 1967 from New York. Making her maiden voyage to New York in secrecy in 1940, she spent her war years as a troopship, before entering commercial service on 16 October 1946.

Bunkering for her return voyage to New York on 21 September 1967, *Queen Elizabeth* is attended to by the 856grt, 1959-built *Esso Hythe*. After a two-day turnaround, the Lizzie sailed for New York on the 22nd.

Her grey hull showing some signs of wear, Port Line's *Port Pirie* is berthed next to the International Cold Store at Berth 108 on 21 September 1967, unloading a cargo of Antipodean beef, lamb and butter. Built in 1947 at Swan Hunter's, she was scrapped in 1972.

As well as the Fyffe's boats, other banana boats would call at the port. Here is the Honduran-registered MV *Almirante* (3,817grt, 1954) on 21 September 1967.

Above and below: Originally the Netherland Line's 1939 *Oranje*, she was sold to Lauro in 1964 along with Rotterdam Lloyd's *Willem Ruys*, and after an extensive rebuild became *Angelina Lauro*. She spent her early years for Lauro sailing on the Australia run. Converted to a full-time cruise ship, she met her end at St Thomas in the Virgin Islands on 20 March 1979 when she caught fire at her berth and was totally gutted. Forty years and twenty day after her maiden voyage on 4 September 1939, she sank en route to the breakers.

Angelina Lauro (top) in the Western Docks on 21 September 1967 and (below) sailing outward bound the following day on a voyage to Australia via the Suez Canal.

Built in 1930 as *Kenya* for British India, she was used as a landing ship during the Second World War. BI refused her back at the end of the war and the Ministry of War Transport acquired *Kenya* (now renamed *Keren*). After a series of owners, she was sold to the Sitmar Line and became *Castel Felice* in 1952. In 1970 she caught fire in Southampton docks and was sold for scrap after her final voyage to Sydney in September 1970. Viewed here while on the Australian emigrant run on 22 September 1967.

One of the most famous visitors to the port was the SS *France*, built in 1961 at St Nazaire for the CGT or French line. Here she is seen outward bound passing Mayflower Park on 18 October 1967. She was sold and became the Norwegian SS *Norway* and last visited the port in 2001 on what was supposedly her last transatlantic trip. After returning to the USA, a boiler explosion saw her return to Bremerhaven where she was laid up for two years until sent to be broken up in India.

A Red Funnel tug in attendance, P&O's *Chusan* has newly arrived at Berth 102 in the Western Docks on 19 November 1967. The brand-new Moroccan MV *El-Hassani*, of 2,673grt, is at Berth 101.

P&O's *Chusan* at Berth 102 and the German motor vessel *Las Palmas* (1,927grt) at Berth 101 on 19 November 1967. Both ships were built in the same year of 1950. This view is from Mayflower Park.

By the late 1960s, the Cunard fleet was being drastically reduced. The golden years were over and even ships built in the mid-1950s were being sold. In January 1968, the *Carinthia* was sold to become the Liberian-registered *Fairland*, after only twelve years service with Cunard. Berthed on her port-side is the laid-up *Caronia*. This view from 8 June 1968 was taken after *Caronia* was sold to Universal Lines Inc. in November 1967, but before she sailed from the port as the re-named *Columbia*.

A small crowd watches as *Oronsay* leaves Southampton on 9 June 1968. Interestingly, at least four have deck chairs and must have been spending a long afternoon at the port watching the shipping traffic.

The Holland America Liner *Maasdam*, of 1952, on 9 June 1968. Originally to be named *Diemerdijk*, she made her maiden voyage from Rotterdam via Le Havre, Southampton and Montreal before reaching New York. On 10 December 1952, she rammed and sank the tanker *Ellen*, with the loss of six lives aboard the smaller ship. In 1954, she was in collision with the French cargo ship *Tofevo*. Sold to Polish Ocean line in 1968, she was renamed *Stefan Batory* and ended her career as an accommodation ship.

Now preserved in Rotterdam, the Holland America Line's *Rotterdam* was built in 1959 and is shown here leaving Southampton on 11 June 1968. She has almost finished a €200M refit into a luxury hotel.

With tugs at her side, the Chandris Line's *Queen Frederica*, originally built in 1927, enters the port on 14 June 1968 before another £10 Assisted Passage to Australia.

One of the finest ships ever to sail for Holland America Line was the Art Deco *Nieuw Amsterdam*. Built in 1938, and extensively used as a troopship for the Dutch Government in Exile and the Allies, she lasted over thirty-five years with the line. This view shows her leaving port on 19 June 1968. In 1967 she had been re-boilered with secondhand boilers from a US Navy vessel and in 1971 became a full-time cruise ship. She was sold for breaking in 1974, still adorned with her original HAL livery.

Cunard are well known for their huge transatlantic liners but they were also a cargo company and had a fleet of smaller cargo ships such as the 1960 *Andania*, shown here on 19 June 1968. She sailed for Cunard until 1969, when she was transferred to Brocklebank, a Cunard subsidiary, and renamed *Macharda*. Shown to her left is *Queen Elizabeth*, which had been sold by Cunard on 5 April 1968, before sailing from the port to Port Everglades in November 1968, after her final transatlantic trip early that month.

The Norwegian *Oslofjord* dressed overall and flying her Blue Peter on 14 June 1968. The 16,923grt liner was built in 1949.

Another two ex-Cunarders were in port on 19 June 1968 too. Shown in the Western Docks are *Fairland* (ex-*Carinthia*) and *Sylvania*, which was to become *Fairwind*. Despite it being over six months since her sale to Sitmar of Genoa, her name and port of registry have yet to be changed. The two ships were to be berthed in Southampton until 1971, when they were towed to Italy for conversion to emigrant ships on the Australian run.

The Bulgarian passenger steamer *Varna* (13,581grt, built 1951) at Southampton on 20 June 1968.

Shaw Savill's SS *Northern Star* was built in 1962 for a round-the-world service but was never that successful a vessel. Viewed in torrential rain leaving Southampton on 7 July 1968.

The Panamanian steamer *Columbia* being readied to leave Southampton for the last time on 28 July 1968. Originally built as Cunard's *Caronia* and entering service on 4 January 1949, she had been sold for further service as a cruise ship and renamed. Laid up in 1970, she was wrecked at Apra in Guam in 1974 on her way to Taiwan for demolition. Broken in three pieces, she was scrapped where she lay.

Orcades berthed and *Oronsay* being pulled out by tugs on 28 July 1968.

Oronsay passes two yachts while outbound on 28 July 1968. She is escorted by a Red Funnel tug.

The British India *Uganda* (16,907grt, 1952) on 28 July 1968.

The fourteen-year-old, London-registered *Iberia*, of P&O, being refueled on 24 August 1968.

Once the flagship of Rotterdam Lloyd, and laid down in 1939 but not entering service until 1947 owing to the war, the *Willem Ruys* was sold in 1964 to Star Lauro and became the *Achille Lauro*. Extensively rebuilt in 1965 after an explosion aboard ship, she became world famous in 1985 when she was captured by Palestinian terrorists and the ship held hostage. In 1994, as *Star Lauro*, she sank off Somalia after catching fire.

Fyffe's SS *Matina* (6,801grt, 1946) unloading bananas on 24 August 1968.

The banana boats were a weekly visitor to the port in the 1950s and 1960s. On 31 August 1968 Fyffe's *Changuinola* (6,095grt, 1957) was unloading her cargo of fruit.

Built in 1955, *Southern Cross* was the more successful of the Shaw Savill duo and survived until quite recently as a cruise ship. She is shown here on 31 August 1968.

An unusual visitor to Southampton was the *Principe Perfeito* of the Companhia Nacional de Navegacaos and was mainly used on their service from Portugal to Southern Africa. Built at Swan Hunter's on the Tyne in 1960, she was sold in 1976 and used as an accommodation ship. Sold in 1980 to Sitmar, she became *Fairsky* but was renamed *Vera* and sold in 1982 to John Latsis, who used her as a pilgrim ship to Mecca. In 2001 she went for breaking at Alang.

The Black Sea Shipping Company's cruise ship MV *Shota Rustaveli* was named after a twelfth-century Georgian poet and entered service in mid-1968, shortly before this view was taken on 13 October 1968. Built in East Germany, she was handed over to Ukraine after the fall of the Soviet Union and was scrapped in 2003 at Alang, India.

Left: Taken from aboard the Hythe ferry, this view shows the future of transatlantic travel on 11 June 1969, a ship which made her belated, and much-delayed, maiden voyage from Southampton on 2 May 1969. This ship was to become the second most famous ship ever to sail from Southampton after the *Titanic*. Her life is one of superlatives but she made her final voyage from Southampton on Armistice Day, 2008, amid a huge fireworks display and hundreds of thousands of well-wishers. Her last day in port was not without its challenges, not least being marooned on a sandbank, thankfully on a rising tide.

Below: The *Queen Elizabeth 2* is shown here off Fawley, being followed out of port by the 1959 MV *Esk Queen* on 13 June 1969. The author was lucky enough to sail on her last Southampton round trip when she was stuck on a sandbank not far from here.

Photographed on 13 August 1969 on a rare visit to Southampton is Moore-McCormack Line's SS *Argentina*. This was her last voyage to Southampton as on 3 September 1969, on her return to Baltimore, Maryland, she was laid up. Sold in 1972 to Holland America Line, she became *Veendam* and sailed for HAL for many years. In December 2003, the last American-built luxury liner was beached at Alang and demolished.

Ordered for Lloyd Triestino in 1960, *Galileo Galilei* entered service on the Italy-Australia route in 1963. Shown here on a rare visit to Southampton on 17 August 1969, she became a cruise ship in 1977 for Italia Crociere and was sold in 1983 to Chandris and renamed *Galileo*. As *Sun Vista*, her engine room caught fire on 20 May 1999 and she sank the following day after all 1,090 passengers and crew were rescued.

The Polish steamer *Stefan Batory*, the ex-*Maasdam* of HAL, outward bound on 20 September 1969. Her maiden voyage as *Stefan Batory* was from Gydnia on 11 April 1969.

Both ex-Cunard liners, *Fairwind* and *Fairland* are berthed at Southampton's Western Docks on 20 September 1969. Constructed by John Brown's on the Clyde, *Fairwind* was originally *Sylvania* and *Fairland* was *Carinthia*. They had been built for the Canadian service but by the mid-1960s were redundant and were sold off for further trading. Both ships remained laid up at Southampton until 1971 before entering Sitmar service.

One of the Union Castle cargo ships, MV *Rochester Castle* was built in 1937, and is shown here on 25 September 1969. She was scrapped in 1970 in Whampoa after a long career, during which she was torpedoed off Malta by German E-boats during the relief of the Island in 1942.

Built as the *Huascaran* in Hamburg as a cargo-liner in 1939, she served as a submarine depot ship for the Germans during the war and was handed to the Canadians to become *Beaverbrae* as war reparation. Sold in 1954 to Cogedar Line for service to Australia, and renamed *Aurelia*, she occasionally made transatlantic voyages too. Rebuilt in 1968 for a Southampton-Madeira service, *Aurelia* could carry 740 passengers and is shown here on 25 September 1969. Sold to Chandris in 1970, she was renamed *Romanzia*. In 1997, after a long career, she caught fire while owned by Paradise Cruises and was sold for scrap to Egypt.

In 2005, after a remarkable sixty-one years of service the American President Line's SS *President Roosevelt* was scrapped in India. She is shown here leaving Southampton on 8 March 1970. Built as the USS *General W.P. Richardson*, she saw service as a troopship in both the Second World War and the Korean War. Soon after this view was taken, she was sold to Chandris Line and renamed *Atlantis*.

The French Line's *Antilles* (19,828grt), built in 1953, leaving Southampton on 4 April 1970.

MV *Rustenburg Castle* (built 1946, 7,767grt) on the Itchen, in front of the Ocean Terminal, on 4 April 1970. She was scrapped in China after being sold for £147,500 in September 1971.

MV *Riebeeck Castle*, 11 April 1970. Launched on 23 October 1945 at Harland & Wolff's as a refrigerated fruit carrier, *Riebeeck Castle* carried general freight southbound. Scrapped in 1971 in Taiwan.

The North German Lloyd MV *Europa* leaving Southampton on 11 April 1970. Built for the Swedish Amerika Line as the *Kungsholm*, she was sold to NDL in 1965 and survived in NDL/Hamburg Amerika ownership until 1981 when she was sailed for Costa Cruises as *Columbus C*. In 1984, she rammed a breakwater in Cadiz and sank. Raised the following year, she was towed to Barcelona for scrapping.

Orient Line's *Orsova* on 11 April 1970, the sea reflected off her starboard side.

Above On 11 April 1970, *Arcadia* was in the Western Docks, with Cunard's *Queen Elizabeth 2* just visible behind her, in the King George V dry dock. With her anchor chain part way down and rope ladders hanging from her side, it looks as if *Arcadia* is getting her anchor chain links painted in white.

Right: Dry-docked for the first time in the King George V dry dock on 11 April 1970 barely a year after her maiden voyage, *QE2* is photographed from an unusual angle.

Berthed in the Western Docks on 20 February 1971 is the 18,655grt SS *Britanis* of the Chandris Line.

Shaw Savill's *Akaroa* (18,565grt, 1959) at Southampton on 14 August 1971. She was renamed soon after as *Akarita* and became Norwegian-registered. Behind is the *SA Vaal*.

Built in France and now with the Saga cruise line as *Saga Rose*, the *Sagafjord* went through various owners from Norwegian American Line through Cunard and finally to Saga, where she ends her life as a cruise ship in 2009. This view, showing both *Sagafjord* and Shaw Savill's *Ocean Monarch* in the Ocean Dock, dates from 25 September 1971. *Ocean Monarch* was built in 1959.

Ocean Monarch (24,467grt, 1957) on 25 September 1971.

The 1954-built *Iberia* of 29,779grt, photographed on 11 May 1972, had but a few short months to live, being sold later that year for scrap. The 1970s were hard on British shipping, with many ships heading for the breaker's yard through a combination of old age, competition from aircraft and the expensive and rising fuel prices of the early 1970s. *Canberra*, behind, was to be a survivor though, managing to last until 1997, when she sailed for Alang and demolition on an Indian beach.

SA Oranje in front of the *Iberia* and *Canberra* on 11 May 1972 in the Western Docks.

The Cia Trasatlantica Espanola purchased the *Castel Bianco*, an Italian emigrant ship which had been built as the *Vassar Victory* in 1945 as one of the American Victory ships, and converted her to the *Begona*, of 10,139grt. Shown here on 11 May 1972, she was scrapped three years later at Castellon.

Windsor Castle has her anchor and chain painted on 11 May 1972. The two-day layover at Southampton allowed much routine maintenance and painting to be done on the vessels that called.

Carmania and *Franconia* getting steam up on 11 May 1972. Sold by Cunard after being laid up in 1971, they were renamed *Leonid Sobinov* and *Fedor Shalyapin* respectively before sailing for Russia.

Above and below: Two views of *Canberra* on 19 August 1972 showing British India's *Nevasa* at her bow and the Orient liner *Orcades* at her stern. Both Orient and British India were subsidiaries of P&O.

The MV *Ardrossan* of 1968 bunkers the *Oriana* on 19 August 1972.

Dressed overall as she is pushed into her berth on 19 August 1972 is the *Orcades*.

British India's *Nevasa* was originally built in 1956 as a troopship at Barclay, Curle's yard on the Clyde. Six years later, trooping by sea was suspended and all future trooping was made by air. In 1966, *Nevasa* was converted to an educational cruise ship, retaining her dormitories, but in 1975 she made her last voyage. Because of the oil crisis she was too expensive to run and re-engining her was considered uneconomical so she was sold for breaking in Taiwan in April of that year.

19 August 1972 at the Southampton Ocean Terminal, which was opened by Clement Attlee in 1950, with the *Chusan*, built in the same year, dressed overall while awaiting her passengers for her next voyage.

The Dutch banana boat SS *Tanamo* (6,276grt, 1947) on 19 August 1972.

Originally built as *Port Sydney* for the Port Line, *Akrotiri Express* is shown here on 19 August 1972, with the *Oriana* ahead of her. She had been sold that year by Port Line and converted to a car ferry. In 1975 she re-entered service as the upmarket cruise ship *Daphne* after a costly rebuild. Still in service as *Ocean Monarch* and often chartered to Page & Moy, she is still a familiar sight in British waters.

The brand-new *Royal Viking Star* with Norwegian American Line's *Sagafjord* astern on 2 September 1972.

In the Ocean Dock on 2 September 1972 were the Greek tanker MV *Stabenko*, built in 1970; the Sitmar liner *Fairsky*, built in 1942 and of 12,464grt; and the Chandris Line's SS *Ellinis*.

Above and below: P&O's first new-build of the 1970s was the 17,370grt *Spirit of London*, a dedicated cruise ship. Here she is on 28 October 1972, with two of her lifeboats being tested and her crew drilled. Ahead of her are two Orient liners, the one immediately ahead being *Oronsay*, with a South African liner ahead of the second Orient ship.

Oronsay and the brand-new *Spirit of London* cruise ship in the Western Docks. The author sailed on *Spirit of London*'s sister ship *Seawing*, for Airtours cruises in 2003. The week after this, Airtours closed its cruise division and *Seawing* was sold on to Louis Cruises.

Photographed on 8 May 1973, all of four days before her final voyage to Taiwanese ship breakers, *Chusan* still looks every part the quintessential British liner, her paint still fresh. Behind her are the *SA Vaal* of 1961 and the *Edinburgh Castle* of 1948, both used on the South African mail run.

One day after *Chusan* sailed to the breakers, her larger sister, *Himalaya*, was in port. Just forward of the bridge, *Himalaya's* huge cargo hatch is open.

Ahead of *Himalaya* on the same day was *Oriana*, being painted with anti-fouling paint along her starboard side.

Being bunkered by *Esso Woolston* and just ahead of *Oriana* was *Orsova*, another Orient liner, dressed overall and ready to sail later that day. *Orsova* had spent a reasonable part of her life on the transpacific route from San Francisco to Australia and was broken for scrap in 1974 after a twenty-year life in Orient and P&O service.

Built in 1964 for ZIM Israel Navigation at St-Nazaire as *Shalom*, and sold to become the *Hanseatic* in 1967, she was sold again to Home Lines and renamed *Doric* in 1973. Laid up in 1995 after her then owners Regency Cruises went bust, she sank on her way to the breaker's yard while off South Africa in 2001. She is shown here on 16 May 1974, on the Ocean Dock soon after entering Home Lines service.

Photographed outside the International Cold Storage Co.'s store is Shaw Savill's *Ionic*. The name was used originally on one of the first White Star Line ships and on a Shaw Savill and White Star joint service to New Zealand. The name was last used on this 1959 ship, shown here on 25 May 1974.

The Pacific Far East Line purchased *Monterey* from the Matson Line in 1970. Built in 1952 as the cargo ship *Pine Tree Mariner*, she was purchased by Matson in 1955 and rebuilt as *Monterey*. By 1955 she was owned by MSC, the Italian cruise line, and was scrapped after her final season in 2006. She is shown here on 25 May 1974 on a rare visit to Southampton's Docks.

The date is 27 July 1975 and the Suez crisis had taken a huge toll on the British merchant marine. Many of the liners shown on the previous pages had been sold for scrap or future trading. By 1980, *Canberra* was responsible for some 50 per cent of all British cruise passengers sailing from Britain, a time when only 150,000 people left Britain on cruises.

The Russian SS *Leonid Sobinov* was originally built on the Clyde for Cunard as *Saxonia* in 1954. She was used for cruising and made occasional UK-Australia voyages. She is shown here on that service on 27 July 1975. Southampton's huge floating crane can be seen to the far right. On 1 April 1999, she reached Alang and was broken up soon afterwards.

The Dutch-registered SS *Toltec* (6,276grt, 1947) leaving Southampton on 17 August 1975.

Photographed slightly over seven months apart, it is amazing just how different a ship can look. The first view shows *Oriana* on 5 October 1975 while the next view shows her again on 16 May 1976, soon before she was sold to China for use as a floating hotel. Her once-pristine white paint is now weathered and she looks far from being the flagship of a major shipping line. More economical and more reliable than *Canberra*, it was strange that *Oriana* should be first to go, but P&O were correct in their judgement and *Canberra* became a firm favourite with the British public until her demise in 1997. *Oriana*, despite leaving service over two decades before *Canberra*, outlasted her, before being sunk in a cyclone and scrapped in 2006.

The German coaster MV *Buxtehude II* (499grt, 1969) and Union Castle's *Edinburgh Castle* in the Western Docks on 5 October 1975.

Three Clan Line ships berthed side by side on 5 October 1975. From left to right are the three sister ships *Clan Ranald* (1965, 7,955grt), *Clan Robertson* (1965) and *Clan Ross* (1966).

Berthed in the Itchen, opposite Vosper Thornycroft's, on 16 May 1976 is the Chandris Line's SS *Ellinis*.

Built in 1974 for Aznar Line's Southampton-Santander car ferry service, the *Monte Toledo* was of 10,839grt and is shown here on 14 August 1976. She was sold in 1977 to a Libyan company, renamed *Garnata*, and is still in service.

The eleven-year-old, Glasgow-registered MV *Kinpurnie Castle* on 5 September 1977.

The Greek cruise ship *Atlas* on 5 September 1977. Originally built in 1951 as the Holland America Line's *Ryndam*, she was sold in 1972 to World Wide Cruises and renamed *Atlas*. In 2003 she was sold for scrap but failed to reach her destination, sinking in the Pacific on her way to India.

CHAPTER 2

The Changing Face of Cargo Ships

The 1960s and 1970s were a period of huge change in cargo shipping. The 1966 Seamen's Strike had all but crippled the British shipping industry and the closure of the Suez Canal to all shipping saw a change in ship design and size. Containerisation had a huge impact on ship design and on trade. Ships could be loaded and unloaded in a matter of a few days rather than upwards of a week as previously.

Some British lines were slow to make the change from traditional ships to container vessels and ports such as Southampton could not cope with the supertankers being built in the aftermath of the Suez Canal's closure.

Southampton continued, though, to have a wide variety of vessels calling all the way through the 1960s and 1970s as evidenced by the images shown here of a wide range of vessels, all using the South Coast's premier port.

Unloading timber on 14 September 1957 is the Dutch MV *Liberty*. Built in 1952 in Groningen in the Netherlands, she was only of 399grt and belonged to EPE & JP Beck.

The *Copsewood* was constructed in Burntisland in 1951 for the Constantine Shipping Co. of Middlesbrough. At 226ft long, she grossed 1,272 tons. Photographed on 2 August 1964 while discharging bulk cargo, the stern of Cunard's *Mauretania* can just be seen behind her.

The Norwegian motor tanker *Polarprins* at Fawley refinery on 14 May 1966. Built in 1955 at Barclay, Curle's at Partick, Glasgow, she belonged to Melsom & Melsom of Larvik and was sold in 1968 to become *Kavo Aetos*. Scrapped in Taiwan in 1973.

On the same day the Norwegian tanker *Torvanger* visited Fawley too. Built in Sunderland in March 1955, she was broken up in 1973 in Yugoslavia.

Above and below: Alva Star (top), a 1953 motor tanker belonging to the Vlasov group, owners of Sitmar Cruises, at Southampton on 21 September 1967. On 23 September 1969, after a name change to *Angel Gabriel* on 22 September 1967, she went ashore at St Thomas Point, Wied-il-Ghajn, Marsascala, Malta, during a severe storm and was a total loss. She broke in two and one crewmember lost his life. Shown here (below) bunkering from *Esso Hythe* after her name change.

The refinery this vessel was named after was opened in 1951 and continues to be one of the most state-of-the-art refineries in the UK. *Esso Fawley* was built in 1967 and is shown here on 18 October of that year.

The Russian MV *Otepya* (1964, 1,248grt) at the Town Quay, surrounded by timber barges, on 8 June 1968. *Oteypa* was built at the Angyalfold Works in Budapest, on the Danube.

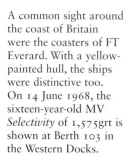

A common sight around the coast of Britain were the coasters of FT Everard. With a yellow-painted hull, the ships were distinctive too. On 14 June 1968, the sixteen-year-old MV *Selectivity* of 1,575grt is shown at Berth 103 in the Western Docks.

Above and below: Two views of the French Line's MV *Rochambeau* (1967/9,848grt) on 28 July 1968. The upper view shows her with the tug North Pole while the lower view shows her with British India Line's *Uganda*. *Uganda* was to go on to play a major part in the Falklands conflict as a hospital ship.

The East German MV *Kormoran* (1963, 1,824grt) on 28 July 1968. Owned by Deutsche Seereederei, she was built by Schiffswerft Neptun.

Esso Lyndhurst, built in Hessle near Hull in 1958, was a common sight in Southampton, bunkering many of the ships which called into the port. Travelling from Fawley into the Western Docks, she is probably bunkering the two P&O liners visible ahead of her on 28 July 1968.

The MV *Calshot* (1964, 494grt) tug and passenger tender and the salvage vessel *Twyford* (1952, 1,104grt) on 24 August 1968. *Twyford* belonged to the local company of Risdon Beazley and was built in Aberdeen. Risdon Beazley's was based at Clausentum yard shown here and undertook yacht repair as well as salvage work.

Built at Goole and launched on 12 December 1962 as Yard No.536 for FT Everard, the MV *William J. Everard* is shown on 13 October 1968 berthed near to Joseph Rank's Solent Flour Mills. She was converted to a drilling ship for Wimpey in 1982 and renamed *Wimpey Geocore*. In 1992 this coaster was in Nigeria as *Ecowas Trader 1*.

Unloading timber at the Town Quay on 7 June 1969 is the German coaster *CH Bohl* (1956, 498grt). The Town Quay is still home to the Red Funnel Isle of Wight ferries today. In the background can be seen the Harland & Wolff ship repair yard, which also housed the Trafalgar Dry Dock.

Shown in the Western Docks on 17 August 1969 is the ex-Wilson Line steamer *Cattaro*, built in 1945 and sold to Panamanian interests in 1967.

A fine view looking into the Ocean Dock showing the port's floating crane as well as the *Changuinola* (1957, 6,095grt) on 25 September 1969.

For a time in the 1970s oil rigs were built at Southampton. The drilling platform *North Star* and Japanese tug *Amaryllis* (1967, 1,811grt) are berthed on 8 March 1970. *North Star* wasn't built in the port, being constructed at Clydebank in 1965. She is currently operating in Brazil and can work in 200ft of water and drills to 18,000ft. Hammond Innes set one of his novels aboard the *North Star* when she was drilling in the North Sea.

Owned by Lykes Bros Steamship Co., the bulkbreak cargo ship *Marjorie Lykes* was built by the Bethlehem Steel Co. in 1962. Of 9,244grt, she was 495ft long and is shown here on 4 April 1970.

More commonly seen on the Thames, this unusual class of vessel was designed to be capable of travelling under many of London's bridges delivering cargo, ordinarily coal or oil (as in this case), to the many small berths above the Pool of London. The MV *Worthing* (1957, 1,873grt) visits Southampton on 2 July 1971.

The dredger *Sand Swift* (1969, 1,162grt) on 10 July 1971, a bare two years after she was built. Unloading sand, she was owned by South Coast Shipping Ltd, which ultimately became part of Cemex UK Marine Ltd. She was sold in 2007 to Portugal as the *Atlantiareia*.

Owned by the New Zealand Shipping Co. and built in 1966 by Bartram & Sons, of Sunderland, the MV *Tekoa* is bunkering from *Esso Lyndhurst* on 11 May 1972. Ahead of the *Esso Lyndhurst*, a painter is out touching up the hull paintwork of *Tekoa*.

The brand-new steam tanker SS *Esso Caledonia* (1971, 126,535grt) was one of the largest vessels to use the port. Within eleven years of her visit to the port on 25 September 1971, she had been scrapped.

The New Zealand Shipping Company's MV *Otaio* was a cadet training ship for NZSC and had accommodation for forty deck cadets and thirty engineering cadets. She performed this role from construction by John Brown's in Clydebank in 1958 until 1975. Powered by two Doxford diesel engines, she had a service speed of 17 knots. She is shown here on 19 August 1972.

Above and below: Esso Woolston and MV *Ardrossan* bunkering P&O's *Oriana* on 19 August 1972. MV *Ardrossan* was built in 1968 and was of 1,529grt.

British Railway's cargo vessel MV *Elk* on 19 August 1972 in the inner docks. Her deck cargo is primarily British Railways containers, designed for transshipment between rail and ship. Ahead of their time, British Railways containers had curved roofs and could not be stacked in the way that TEU containers could be and they were phased out in the 1970s. Just over a month after this view was taken Southampton had closed as a railway port and this was one of the last sailings that the 1959 *Elk* made from the port.

The French refrigerated cargo ship MV *Marsouin* berthed at the Fyffe's Bananas terminal on 28 October 1972. Built in 1969 and of 8,570grt, she was launched in Dunkirk and was fitted with Burmeister & Wain diesel engines giving her a top speed of 15.5kt. Broken up at Alang in 2003 after a long career with at least eight different names.

The West German MV *Teutonia* was built in 1972 and is shown here the year after on 13 May. By 1973 more and more cargo was being transported by container. New cranes were needed to cope with the containers but their use speeded up freight handling considerably.

French-registered but part of the Atlantic Container Line group (a consortium of shipping lines including Cunard and the French Line), the MV *Atlantic Cognac* (1970, 15,351grt) is shown here on 13 May 1973 at the container terminal. The huge cranes are offloading her cargo of containers.

The Leith-registered MV *Benalder* laden with containers on 16 May 1974. At 58,840grt she was one of the largest British container ships at the time and could carry 2,687 TEU containers.

At 31,036grt, the Bristol-registered MV *Dart America* was owned by Clarke Traffic Services of Montreal, but operated by Dart Container Line, in itself part-owned by Bristol City Line. By 25 May 1974, when this view was taken, the line had been purchased by Bibby Line of Liverpool. Already the size of container ships was getting larger and there are now vessels which can carry over 10,000 TEU containers.

At Berth 39 is the two-year-old *Iris Queen* on 25 May 1974. The photographer is being stared out, it seems, by the man under the bow of *Iris Queen*.

Already thirty-three years old, the MV *Margaret Smith* was built in 1943 and is shown on 11 May 1976.

VIC62, a wartime Victualling Inshore Craft, built to a typical Clyde Puffer design, was 85ft long and had a cargo capacity on 100 tons. She is shown here in her coasting role on 11 May 1976 but was, until recently, used to dredge seaweed in the Fal estuary. Numerous VICs survive today.

The 41,521grt motor tanker *Lord Mount Stephen* was built in 1966 but had been laid up until 4 April 1976. She is shown here while on charter to Shell on 11 May 1976, rust-streaked, paint flaking from her superstructure. Having left dry dock she was still being readied for service when this photo was taken in the Western Docks. Her charter was to North Sea oil rigs to load with oil and then drop it at numerous UK ports.

At Berth 103 is Royal Mail Lines' MV *Drina* on 16 May 1976. Built in 1953 for Shaw Savill as *Cymric*, she was transferred to RML in 1972. In December 1978, the 10,961grt vessel reached Kaohsiung, Taiwan, for breaking.

8 August 1976 and Blue Star Line's MV *Brasilia Star* unloads a cargo from South America. Originally built for the Australian route by the Fairfield Shipbuilding & Engineering Co. in 1957 as Yard No.779, she was renamed *Brasilia Star* in 1972 when she transferred to the South American route. She made her final voyage from Newhaven in Sussex to Taiwan for demolition on 16 November 1979.

CHAPTER 3

Red Funnels & Other Ferries

Southampton has always been an important ferry port, not just for the Isle of Wight but also for France and the Channel Islands. One mustn't forget the Hythe ferry and the venerable small ships which have made that journey their own too. The most well-known and certainly longest lasting of any of the ferry companies in the UK is the Southampton, Isle of Wight & South of England Royal Mail Steam Packet Company. This line, with the longest name of any registered British company, is well known to us all today as Red Funnel and they still operate a service from the Town Quay to Cowes. Southampton, in the 1960s and 1970s, saw a resurgence in ferry travel with ships sailing to destinations as far away as Madeira and the Canaries in the summer, as well as year-round journeys to France and the Isle of Wight.

Above: The Thoresen ferry MV *Viking II* (1964, 3,611grt) leaving Southampton on 21 May 1966 en route to Cherbourg. She was occasionally chartered to Lion Ferry and Stena Line but was sold in 1976 to Sealink and renamed *Earl William*.

Left: Sixty years young in 2009 is the MV *Balmoral*, a true Southampton survivor. She has spent more time away from the port now than when in her Red Funnel years, having left for Bristol in 1969, but she is still a regular visitor in the summer. She is berthed at the Town Quay on 20 July 1966.

With *Queen Mary* in the background, Red Funnel's *Carisbrooke Castle* brings two lorries to Southampton from East Cowes on 20 July 1966. Built by Thorneycroft's in 1959, she was withdrawn in 1974 and sold for use between Naples and Ischia for Societa Partenopea di Navigazione S.p.A., Naples, and renamed *Citta di Meta*. This company sold her in 1989 for service between Porto S. Stefano and the Isola del Giglio. In 1990, named *Giglio Expresso II*, she was sold to Transporti Regionali Marittimi of Naples, for services between Calasetta and Carloforte.

Swedish Lloyd's MV *Patricia* was built specifically for the Southampton to Bilbao service in 1967. She is shown here at Southampton's ferry terminal on 20 September 1967. After numerous name changes, she became *Amusement World* in 1998 and now sails regularly from Penang on gambling cruises.

Normandy Ferries was formed in 1967 in a joint venture between P&O's General Steam Navigation Co. and France's S.A.G.A. The two ships, one British (*Dragon*), the other French (*Leopard*), ran from Southampton to Le Havre. *Dragon* is shown here leaving Southampton on 14 June 1968.

Balmoral was built in Southampton, at Thorneycroft's yard in Woolston in 1949, replacing some of Red Funnel's tonnage lost during the Second World War. She is now preserved and operates as a pleasure steamer around Britain's coasts. Shown here at the Town Quay on 14 June 1968 in her last full season on the Isle of Wight run.

Fitting out at Woolston on 31 August 1968 is Red Funnel's newest ferry, *Norris Castle*. Her hull is being painted while her windows still have to be fitted. Lifeboat derricks stand empty while two flags fly from her mast. Radar and all other deck equipment is still to be fitted.

A rather cloudy and overcast 31 August 1968 with MV *Viking III* in Southampton.

Norris Castle berthed on 7 June 1969. She was the third vessel to carry the name in Red Funnel service and was rebuilt in Belgium in 1975 with a drive-through arrangement which meant vehicles could drive on and drive off. In 1994 *Norris Castle* was sold to Jadrolinija, of Rijeka, and subsequently named *Lovrjenac*.

Viking I (1964, 3,657grt) was built in Norway by Kaldnes Mekaniske Verksted A/S, Tönsberg, for Otto Thoresen for the ferry service between Southampton and Cherbourg. Shown here on 13 August 1969, she was renamed *Viking Victory* in 1976 when she inaugurated a new service from Portsmouth to Le Havre/Cherbourg. Soon after the other services from Southampton were relocated to Portsmouth. Sold to Cypriot owners in 1983, she has served on various routes in the Aegean, Adriatic and Mediterranean.

Above: The Blue Funnel company was formed in 1957 with the amalgamation of three companies, which operated from Royal Pier. Their boats were inadequate for the popular round-the-docks cruises and so a series of Gosport-Portsmouth ferries were bought. Here, *Venus* (1947, 74grt) is leaving Hythe Pier on 17 August 1969.

Right: Solent Queen (1918, 49grt) at Hythe Pier on 20 September 1969. *Solent Queen* was originally named *Ferry King.*

The Hythe ferry *Hotspur IV* was built by Rowhedge Ironworks in 1946 and is here at the end of Hythe Pier (top) on 20 September 1969. At the time, she was capable of 8.5kt but was re-engined and her top speed raised to 9.5kt. She can carry 300 passengers and is 64ft long.

The bottom image shows *Hotspur IV* in Southampton's docks on the same day. A ferry has existed at Hythe for centuries but the pier was opened in 1881 and has seen a ferry service since that date.

The 786grt *Cowes Castle* on 8 March 1970 with the Gulf Oil drilling platform *Gulftide* in the background. *Cowes Castle* lasted in Red Funnel service until 1994, and had been converted to a drive-through ferry in 1975. *Gulftide* has seen service around the world and is currently off the West coast of Africa.

Blue Funnel's pleasure ship MV *Varos* (1921, 48grt) tied up at the Town Pier on 8 March 1970, with American President Line's SS *President Roosevelt* in the background, having set sail from the Western Docks.

4 April 1970 sees *Hotspur III* tied up at Hythe. She was built by Rowhedge Ironworks in 1938 and was re-engined in 1949 and 1971. Scrapped in 1981 due to a corroded keel, her 1971 engines live on in the *New Forester*.

The *Leopard*, built in 1968, is shown here on 6 April 1971 leaving Southampton for Le Havre. In 1980, P&O dropped the Normandy Ferries name and all ferries became part of P&O Ferries. *Leopard* remained French, however, with a French crew. Since 2002 *Leopard* has sailed as *Talya I* between Brindisi and Cesme.

The German-registered freight ferry MV *Falcon* (1971, 1,599grt) leaving Southampton's ferry terminal on 6 April 1971.

Dragon (1967, 6,141grt) and the Thoresen ferry *Viking IV* (1967, 1,152grt) on 10 April 1971 at the ferry terminal in Southampton. Brand-new cars are lined up beside *Viking IV*, ready to be exported. As shown here, *Viking IV* was in a fetching red livery and was used on the Southampton-Cherbourg freight service. She subsequently moved to the Dover-Zeebrugge route and was sold in 1981.

MV *Varos* at the Town Pier on 2 July 1971.

Eagle, shown here on 25 May 1974, entered service in 1971 on a new cruise ferry service from Southampton to Lisbon and Tangier and belonged to Southern Ferries, owned by the General Steam Navigation Co. In 1975 *Eagle* was sold to Nouvelle Cie. de Paquebots, Marseille (Paquet) and renamed *Azur*. In 1981, *Azur* was rebuilt as a fulltime cruise ship, with cabins replacing the car decks. Sold to Chandris in 1987, and re-named *The Azur*, she was sold to Festival Cruises in 1994. Festival became bankrupt in 2004 and the ship was sold again to Israeli Mano Shipping to become *Royal Iris*. To her stern is the Danish MV *Lindinger Facet* (1973, 1,599grt).

Netley Castle, shown here in her early black-hulled livery, was built by Ryton Marine Ltd, Wallsend-on-Tyne, in 1974, for Red Funnel. She is shown here in the middle of a summer season on 3 August 1975. In 1997 *Netley Castle*, like other Red Funnel ferries, was sold to Jadrolinija, Rijeka, Croatia, and renamed *Sis*. She still serves as a ferry in the Aegean.

Cowes Castle leaves Southampton for East Cowes on 16 May 1976. This view shows her in drive-through form. She still exists as the Croatian ferry *Nehaj* in Rijeka, having been withdrawn from Red Funnel service in 1994.

The 1929 *Verda*, 48grt, tied up at the Town Quay on 25 June 1978. By the end of the 1970s, fewer passenger ships were using the port, it having lost most of its regular sailings by lines such as Union Castle, P&O and Cunard. Cruises had not yet taken off in the way they would do from the mid-1980s onwards.

CHAPTER 4

Cables, Tugs, Explorers & Small Ships

As well as the large liners, cruise ships and cargo vessels which use a port like Southampton, there are also a wide variety of types of vessels seen in and around the port. Some of these ships are always there, like the tugs scuttling around each large vessel that enters or leaves, hustling and bustling round their sterns or bows, nudging them into their berths and generally making themselves look busy. Others, like cable ships, spend most of their time at sea, ensuring we can make our telephone calls and that information flows around the world and only call into port to restock with cable and supplies. Southampton, home to STC, made many of the submarine cables which were loaded onto the cable ships there. Others, like the Royal Research Ships spend much time in the frozen Polar regions, occasionally visiting home, but rarely staying for long before they are victualled and re-crewed. Pleasure boats call too – for refit work or to see the port. Whatever they are doing, they help make any port more interesting and provide a visual feast of variety for the ship enthusiast.

The first reliable transatlantic cable was laid in the 1860s, by Brunel's *Great Eastern*, from Ireland to Newfoundland, and from that date we have needed cable ships to lay new cables and to repair and maintain the ones already laid. By 1967, the ships had become very sophisticated and here the cable ships *Recorder* (1954, 3,349grt) and *Mercury* (1962, 8,962grt) are photographed from Mayflower Park as they lie at Berth 101 on 18 October of that year. Cable & Wireless owned the *Mercury* and *Recorder*.

Many of the cable ships were British but the turbo-electric-powered cable vessel *Long Lines* was an American-owned cable ship. Built in 1963, she was of 11,326grt and is shown here five years after she entered service on 14 June 1968. Belonging to AT&T, she had a crew of seventy and cost $19M when she was constructed.

The Canadian, diesel-electric cable-repair ship and icebreaker *John Cabot* (1965, 5,097grt) at Southampton on 17 August 1969. With her red hull, she was quite a distinctive vessel. *John Cabot* was severely damaged by fire in 1974 and was subsequently refitted. Going through various owners, she is now operated by Italcable in the Mediterranean, laying cables manufactured by Pirelli.

The British cable steamer *Stanley Angwin* on 11 May 1972. After a twenty-year career, she sailed for Belgium to be broken up only three days after this photograph was taken. Named after a Cable & Wireless chairman and built at Swan Hunter's she served most of her life in Singapore before being laid up in March 1971. Despite over a year's lay up she still looks well-cared for in this view.

The Cable & Wireless-owned *CS Mercury* loading cable at Southampton on 13 April 1974.

Above and below: On 3 August 1975, both berths for cable ships were full, with CS *Iris* (top) and CS *Ariel* (below), both loading cables. The cables had to be loaded carefully to avoid any damage. CS *Iris* was built in 1939 and CS *Ariel* in 1940 – the important work of cable-laying and repair never stopped and cable ships were even more important in war time.

Behind CS *Ariel* is the West German steamer *Hamburg Express* (1972, 58,088grt).

The tug *Lady Howard* (1968, 152grt) and the survey vessel MV *John Biscoe* (1956, 1,584grt) on 13 August 1968.

Built in 1960 at Thorneycroft's and in Red Funnel service until 1969, the *Gatcombe* is shown here on 16 August 1967. She was replaced in 1970 by a new *Gatcombe*.

Built by Richard Dunston at Hessle in 1965, the 173grt *Ventnor* takes a rest between two of the huge Stothert & Pitt cranes on 17 August 1969. She was sold by Alexandra Towing Co. to Ward Tugs to become *Sea Vigilant*.

Using a famous name from the 1930s, the second *Calshot* was built in 1964 for Red Funnel as a replacement for the passenger tender and tug *Calshot (I)* of 1930. She survived in Red Funnel service until 1985. *Calshot (I)* is now back in Southampton, having spent many years in Ireland as the *Galway Bay*.

The 1961 Red Funnel tug *Thorness* (247grt) on 14 August 1971.

The Alexandra Towing Co. had many tugs at Southampton, including *Nelson* and *Trafalgar*, as well as the tugs shown on these pages. Here *Brockenhurst* is passing the Town Quay on 19 August 1972.

Romsey (1964, 173grt) on 27 July 1975. She was a familiar sight in the port throughout the 1960s and 1970s.

Behind the tugs *Chale* (1965, 254grt) and *Dunnose* (1958, 241grt) is the auxiliary training ship *Sir Winston Churchill* (1966, 218grt) on 3 August 1975.

The Research Ship *Shackleton* on 24 August 1968. Originally built as the MV *Arendal (III)* in 1955, she was purchased by the Falklands Islands Dependency Survey the same year and refitted with more passenger accommodation. Hitting an iceberg in 1957, she was nearly lost and in 1982 she was shelled during the Falklands conflict. Retired in 1983, she still sails as the seismic survey vessel *Sea Profiler* for Gardline Shipping Ltd.

Built in Aberdeen in 1962, the RRS *Discovery* is shown here on 28 October 1972. With berths for twenty-eight scientists and the ability to spend forty-five days at sea at a time, she was until 1996 the largest research ship in Britain. She had a major overhaul in 1996 which added an extra ten metres to her length. Still in service, she is due to be replaced soon.

Above: The RRS *Bransfield* was the main supply ship for the British Antarctic Survey from her construction in 1970 until she was sold in 1999. Sold when replaced by RRS *Sir Ernest Shakleton*, she provided a valuable service for the British scientists in the Antarctic.

Left: An unknown motor yacht passes one of the Hythe ferries on 25 September 1969.

The motor yacht *Chimon* on 13 April 1974. Registered in Nassau, she was constructed in 1938 and was of 505grt.

Inside the Inner Docks are the MVs *Wilbernia* (1960, 93grt) and the *Wilbonnie* (1956, 71grt) on 13 April 1974.

Photographed in the outer docks on 3 August 1975 is the 1938 MY *Shemara*. She is now owned by Harry Hyams but was owned by Lady Docker in the 1950s and was the site of many fancy parties. For many years, the 212ft *Shemara* (1938, 878grt) lay at Lowestoft docks.

CHAPTER 5

The White Ensign

With a major naval base less than twenty miles away, Southampton has rarely been home for many navy vessels. During both wars, however, the port was a major naval base, especially on the run-up to D-Day. Post-war, while there has often been a naval vessel or two in port, it has been the shipbuilders Thorneycroft, at Woolston, that have been the main reason for there to be navy ships in port. All the way through the 1960s and 1970s, a steady stream of small navy ships left the shipyard for navies the world over.

Many fleet auxiliaries have been based in Southampton and the grey hulls were a common sight, as were US navy ships too.

Above and below: HMS *Abdiel* (top) fitting out at Woolston on 6 August 1967. This exercise minelayer was launched on 22 January 1967 and was designed to lay exercise minefields. She was commissioned on 17 October 1967.

Almost a year later (bottom) on 20 June 1968 and HMS *Abdiel* (N21) is back at Thorneycroft's, with the Libyan naval vessel *Zeltin* behind her. HMS *Abdiel* had a major refit in 1978 and was paid off and sold in 1988 after twenty years in service.

Above and below: The Libyan naval vessel *Zeltin* fitting out on 24 August 1968 (top) and almost completed on 13 October 1968. With a small dry dock in her stern, *Zeltin* was a maintenance repair ship for small patrol craft. She displaces 2,470 tons and is 324ft long. It is thought that she is being used as a hulk now.

The RFA *Sir Tristram* (1967, 4,473grt) on 31 August 1968. Built for the army as a Landing Ship Logistics, she transferred to the Royal Navy in 1970. Damaged severely in the Falklands at Fitzroy, she was brought home on a heavy lift ship and rebuilt. *Sir Tristram* was finally decommissioned in 2005 but is still used for training purposes.

Originally launched as HMS *Sluys* in 1945 and commissioned on 30 September 1946, this view shows her as the Iranian destroyer *Artemiz* on 17 August 1969. Her superstructure was modified when she was sold to Iran in 1967. Still in existence as the destroyer *Damavand* but is currently not active.

The Iranian Navy's *Faramarz* at Woolston on 2 July 1971. Built as part of an order for four vessels, *Faramarz* was a Vosper Mk5 frigate of the Alvand class. Displacing 1,100 tons, she was renamed *Sahand* after the Iranian revolution. She was destroyed by the US Navy during Operation *Praying Mantis* on 18 April 1988.

Above and below: HMS *Amazon*, shown here fitting out on 10 July 1971 was the first of the Type 21 frigates built for the Royal Navy. Suffering a fire in 1977, she highlighted the problems with aluminium superstructures on navy ships. The only one of her class not to serve in the Falklands, she was sold on for further service in September 1993. Purchased by Pakistan, she was renamed *Babur* and still remains in Pakistani service.

Based in Portsmouth for most of her thirty-seven years, HMS *Fearless* was a rare visitor to Southampton on 17 July 1971. Designed as a Landing Platform Dock, she was capable of providing support to a Royal Marines amphibious assault force and also provided a platform for the headquarters capability prior to, and during, the assault phase. Utilised in the Falklands, she saw sterling service in the South Atlantic and was decommissioned in 2002. Scrapped in Belgium after arriving there in December 2007.

With a Ford Anglia on the dockside, HMS *Salisbury* is berthed on 11 May 1972. Built at Devonport Dockyard as a Type 61 aircraft direction frigate, she was laid down on 1 January 1952, launched on 25 June 1953, and handed over on 27 February 1957. Involved in the Cod War in Iceland, she collided with various Icelandic fishing boats. Between 1980-85 she was a training ship and was sunk as a target on 30 September 1985.

Above and middle: Three US vessels were in port on 17 July 1971. Top are the two US Coast Guard cutters *Hamilton* and *Absecon* while below is the USNS *Dutton*. Twelve cutters of the Hamilton class were built at a cost of $16-20M each and they were the largest ships built for the US Coast Guard. With a length of 378ft and the ability to deploy helicopters, the ships are normally to be seen in the Alaskan fishing grounds and used as maritime law enforcement vessels. Dutton was a survey ship, converted from the Victory ship SS *Tuskegee Victory* and scrapped after a long career in 2007.

The new navy vessels *Wilton*, *Dat Assawari* (a Libyan frigate) and *Amazon* at Thorneycroft's on 11 May 1972.

HMS *Fearless* in the Western Docks on 17 July 1971, her landing craft visible on her starboard side.

Fitting out at Thorneycroft's is Type 21 frigate HMS *Active* on 3 August 1975. Launched in November 1972, she did not enter service until 1977. After a long career, in which she operated in the Falklands and suffered hull cracking, she was sold to Pakistan in 1994 and renamed *Shah Jahan*.

On 5 September 1975, the navy presence in Southampton included the Landing Ship Logistics *Sir Geraint* (1967, 4,473grt). She is berthed next to the steamer *Empire Gull* (1945, 4,258grt) and the tanker *Beresford* (1959, 304grt).